JAMES MADISON
OUR FOURTH PRESIDENT

by Ann Graham Gaines

This is a free sample from the series

PRESIDENTS OF THE U.S.A.

www.childsworld.com ★ phone: 800-599-7323 ★ fax: 507-385-1026

THE CHILD'S WORLD ®

Published in the United States of America

The Child's World®
1980 Lookout Drive • Mankato, MN 56003-1705
800-599-READ • www.childsworld.com

Acknowledgments
The Child's World®: Mary Berendes, Publishing Director

The Creative Spark: Mary McGavic, Project Director; Shari Joffe, Editorial
Director; Deborah Goodsite, Photo Research; Nancy Ratkiewich, Page Production

The Design Lab: Kathleen Petelinsek, Design

Content Adviser: Christian J. Cotz, Student Education Coordinator, James
Madison's Montpelier

Photos
Cover and page 3: Collection of the New York Historical Society, USA/The
Bridgeman Art Library International

Interior: Alamy: 25 (North Wind Picture Archives); AP Photo: 20 and 39 right;
The Art Archive: 12 (Chateau de Blerancourt/Dagli Orti); Art Resource: 17
(National Portrait Gallery, Smithsonian Institution); Belle Grove Plantation: 5 left,
5 right; The Bridgeman Art Library: 36 and 39 left (Collection of the New York
Historical Society, USA); Corbis: 8, 10, 27, 30, 31, 37 (Bettmann), 26, 28 and
38 bottom (Francis G. Mayer); Getty Images: 13 (MPI); The Granger Collection:
11; The Image Works: 4 (Roger-Viollet), 34 (Lee Snider); iStockphoto: 44
(Tim Fan); Library of Congress Prints and Photographs Division: 9, 32; Maine
Historical Society: 23; Courtesy The Montpelier Foundation: 14 and 38 top;
North Wind Picture Archives: 7 (North Wind); Photo Researchers, Inc.: 19
(Aaron Haupt); Stock Montage: 22; SuperStock, Inc.: 16, 33 (SuperStock); U.S.
Air Force photo: 45.

Library of Congress Cataloging-in-Publication Data
Gaines, Ann.
James Madison / by Ann Graham Gaines.
    p. cm. — (Presidents of the U.S.A.)
Includes bibliographical references and index.
ISBN 978-1-60253-033-1 (library bound : alk. paper)
1. Madison, James, 1751-1836—Juvenile literature. 2. Presidents—
United States—Biography—MJuvenile literature. I. Title.
E342.G249 2008
973.5'1092—dc22

[B]

2007042599

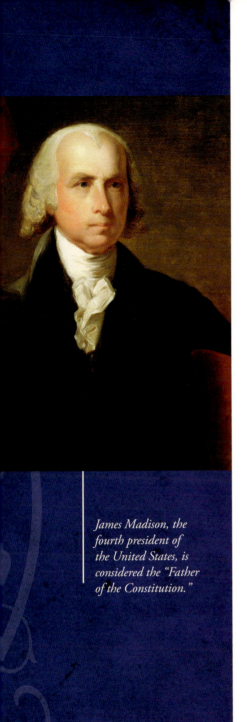

James Madison, the fourth president of the United States, is considered the "Father of the Constitution."

TABLE OF CONTENTS

CHAPTER ONE

A THOUGHTFUL LEADER

James Madison was the fourth president of the United States. When he became president in 1809, he faced difficult challenges. Twenty years earlier, he had been responsible for helping to write the **Constitution,** which created our **federal** government. This was a tremendous source of pride for him. So it was heartbreaking for him when his very young country became involved in a new fight with Great Britain: the War of 1812.

James Madison was born on March 16, 1751. His parents had twelve children, five of whom died very young. James was their oldest child. The Madisons lived on what was then the frontier in the colony of Virginia. They owned a large tobacco **plantation** called Montpelier (mont-PEEL-yur). Like other planters, James Madison's father owned many slaves. They labored in his fields and in the mansion he had built.

James Madison worked for almost 50 years to keep the nation strong and united.

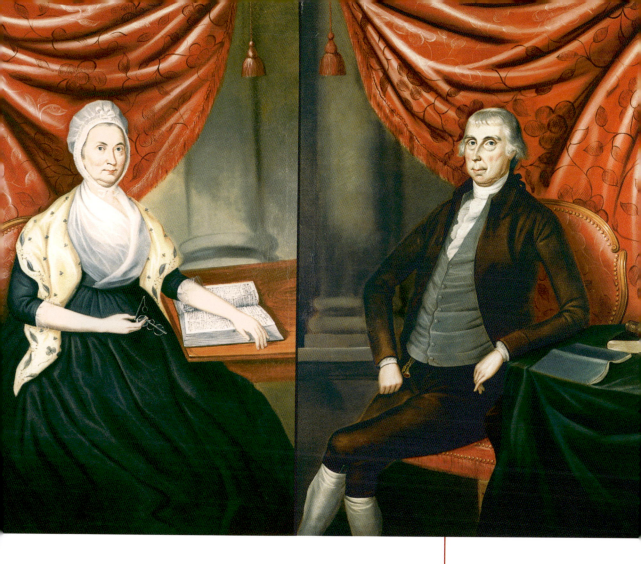

James was often sick when he was a boy. He had to stay inside a lot. Doctors said something was wrong with his liver. He also had what he called "falling sickness," which he thought was **epilepsy.** Sometimes he collapsed with frightening seizures.

There was no school near Montpelier, so Mr. and Mrs. Madison taught their young children at home. The family owned many books. James had read all of them by the time he was 11 years old. Then his parents sent him away to attend a boarding school. When James was 16, his father hired a tutor to teach

James Madison's father (right), also named James, was a successful planter. Madison's mother (left), Nelly Conway Madison, lived at Montpelier until her death at age 97.

At five foot four, James Madison was the shortest U.S. president. He probably weighed the least, too, at just 100 pounds.

the Madison children at home. James then returned to Montpelier to take his lessons.

In 1769, James Madison enrolled at the College of New Jersey (later renamed Princeton University). He hungered for knowledge and learning but still found time for fun. He and his friends liked to play pranks and talk in their rooms until late at night. They had conversations about all kinds of things, but their favorite subject was **politics.** Around that time, Great Britain had ordered colonists to pay new taxes, but they would not allow Americans to have a **representative** in the English government. Madison and his friends believed this was unfair. Many colonists shared this opinion.

It usually took students four years to finish their college studies. Madison studied so hard, he finished in just two years. But all this effort was not without its price. Madison became so sick that he could not attend his graduation. Then he had to stay in New Jersey for one whole year before he felt well enough to travel back to Virginia. The year was not unhappy, though, for Madison spent his time doing the things he liked best—reading, writing, and talking. When he spent times with friends, they still discussed politics. The colonies teetered at the edge of a **revolution,** and Madison believed Americans should fight for independence from England.

At age 22, Madison finally returned to Montpelier. His family's wealth meant that he did not need a job. So he took over the task of teaching his brothers

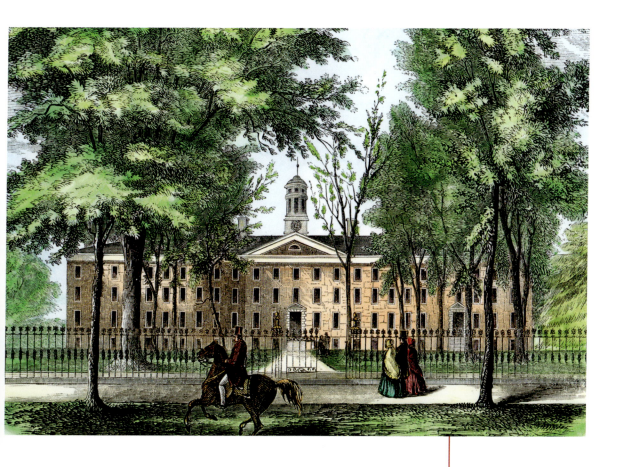

and sisters. He studied law books in his spare time. Madison never became a lawyer, but he did use what he learned from those books. The information helped him understand how to present a good argument. Once he used his law training to help a group of ministers who had been sent to jail. They were punished for preaching their own views instead of what the Church of England told them to say. James Madison believed in religious freedom, which meant people should be able to practice religion in any way they wanted. He would fight for this **ideal** all his life.

Even though he was sickly, Madison studied hard enough to graduate from the College of New Jersey (today's Princeton University) in two years.

The first battle of the Revolutionary War was fought at Lexington, Massachusetts, on April 19, 1775.

According to the laws of the day, only landowners could vote and run for office. In 1774, James Madison bought land so that he could vote. Soon he decided to play a role in the government. Voters elected him to his county's Committee of Safety. This group, which was led by Madison's father, was in charge of making sure the people of the area were ready for war with England. It formed a **militia,** or citizen's army. Madison joined this militia. The Revolutionary War finally broke out in 1775, and Madison wanted to fight. But he still wasn't healthy enough for such a life. Even so, he would make important contributions to the revolutionary effort.

During his second year at college, Madison slept only five hours a night so he would have enough time for all of his studies.

Americans from each colony had to decide if they truly wanted independence. In May of 1776, Madison attended the Virginia Revolutionary **Convention.** The people at this meeting sent a message to the **Continental Congress,** telling its members to vote for independence. They also wrote a new constitution for Virginia.

It was at this meeting that Madison became friends with Thomas Jefferson. Together they wrote the part of the constitution that guaranteed the people of Virginia religious freedom. Madison was still a shy young man, but he had begun to speak out much more in public. He often stood up at these meetings to explain quietly but firmly what he thought the constitution should say. Madison was not one to boast, but later he did say how proud he was to have helped create that important document.

In 1777, Madison was asked to join the Governor's Council, which was an important part of Virginia's

A portrait of James Madison at age 32

Thomas Jefferson and James Madison became good friends. This illustration shows Jefferson (left) and James Madison (right) discussing the site of the future capital.

In 1777, James Madison ran for the Virginia legislature but lost the election. Some people said he lost because he did not buy beer or whiskey for voters to drink after they cast their ballots, which was a common practice at the time.

government during the war years. Thomas Jefferson served as governor. He and Madison continued to find they shared many interests. They both loved to read, write, and talk about ideas. Jefferson came to depend on Madison for advice.

In 1779, Madison was elected to the Continental Congress. For a time, Madison was the youngest **delegate** to Congress. Even so, he soon gathered the respect of his fellow members of Congress. He became known as a great thinker who could solve problems. In 1781, the leader of the British army in the United States surrendered to American general George Washington. This ended the war, although a peace treaty would not be signed for two more years.

Madison remained in Congress after the Revolution was over. By then, the new nation was governed by the **Articles of Confederation.** Madison thought this document was a terrible plan because it gave the states more power than the federal government had. Madison and other leaders wanted to find a way to make the nation's government stronger. They worried that without a united leadership, the country might fall apart. For a time, however, they did not know what to do.

The Revolutionary War ended when British General Charles Cornwallis surrendered to General George Washington at Yorktown, Virginia, on October 19, 1781.

Madison lived at his childhood home, Montpelier (above), throughout much of his adult life, but his involvement in American government meant that he often had to leave home.

Madison's term in Congress ended in 1783. He went home to Montpelier, but he would not stay there for long. The new nation needed its brightest leaders to help decide its fate. In 1784, Madison was elected to the Virginia legislature, the group of people who made the state's laws. As a legislator, he fought against the creation of a tax that would be used to support the church. He also continued to look for ways to help build cooperation between the 13 new states. One issue that representatives from each state argued about was **commerce,** or trade. This worried Madison. In 1785, he suggested that delegates from every state meet to talk about the problems they were having.

The meeting was held in Annapolis, Maryland. It was not a success in that it was not very well attended. The men who did attend, however, did one very important thing. They decided the time had come to change the way the American government worked. They wanted "to render the constitution of the Federal Government adequate to the exigencies [urgent needs] of the Union." In other words, they knew it was time to make changes to the Articles of Confederation. The result would be the U.S. Constitution.

James Madison had a very quiet voice. At meetings, people found it difficult to hear him. Still, audiences listened with attention when he delivered his passionate-but-quiet speeches.

In 1784, Madison was elected to the Virginia state legislature, which met in Richmond (below).

MONTPELIER

Montpelier was the place James Madison called home throughout his life. Located in Orange County, Virginia, this house was built by Madison's father on land that had been in the Madison family for many years. One of the things that made it very special was its view of the scenic Blue Ridge Mountains. The family moved into the house when James Madison was nine. At that time, it was the finest building in the county.

James Madison would spend long periods of time away from Montpelier, first at school and then pursuing his political career. But he always loved to return home to have work done on the house and supervise the farm. He inherited Montpelier in 1801. He and his wife Dolley lived there from 1817 on, after his presidency was over. After Madison's death, Dolley sold the estate. The National Trust for Historic Preservation obtained it in 1984. Recently, the mansion has been restored. It's a popular place for visitors.

CHAPTER TWO

FATHER OF THE CONSTITUTION

After the meeting at Annapolis, a message was sent to each state, asking them to send delegates to what would become known as the Constitutional Convention. This convention began in Philadelphia on May 14, 1787.

The people of Virginia elected several men to represent them at the Constitutional Convention. James Madison was their leader. He would be a very important person there. In fact, he played such a big role that he is often called "The Father of the Constitution." Even before he got to Philadelphia, Madison had thought a lot about how a government should work. He was prepared to tell the delegates what he believed the Constitution should say. After George Washington was elected chairman of the convention and meetings began in earnest, shy Mr. Madison gave many very exciting speeches.

Madison brought a document with him called the Virginia Plan. It said that the delegates from Virginia believed the nation needed a strong central government. It also said the federal government should

George Washington (standing at right with papers) was named chairman of the Constitutional Convention, and he worked hard to make the delegates listen to each other. Sometimes they had terrible arguments, but finally they agreed on what the Constitution should say.

George Washington and James Madison were the only signers of the Constitution who became U.S. presidents.

have more power than the states. The plan became the basis of the Constitution. It proposed the start of a federal government with three parts—the **executive,** the **judicial,** and the **legislative** branches. Madison also suggested the system of **checks and balances,** which made sure that none of the three branches could have too much power.

The convention delegates argued for months. They finally adopted the Constitution on September 17, 1787. Many ideas in the document were those of James Madison.

After the delegates voted to accept the Constitution, it had to be accepted by the states. This meant the delegates went back home to persuade the citizens of their states to vote in favor of the Constitution. This was not a sure thing. James Madison once again played a very important role in **ratification.** To help convince people to vote to ratify the Constitution, he and two other politicians, Alexander Hamilton and John Jay, wrote a series of 85 newspaper articles. Together, they were called the Federalist Papers. People found them interesting and persuasive. It took a long time, but in 1789, the Constitution was ratified.

Once the Constitution was ratified, a new federal government was created with a president, a vice president, and a new Congress. The first president of

James Madison kept a very detailed journal during the Constitutional Convention. It's the best record modern Americans have of what went on there, day by day.

While Thomas Jefferson (left) was in France, he sent Madison books about various forms of government. This information proved helpful as Madison helped craft the Constitution.

Madison worked with Alexander Hamilton to write *The Federalist Papers,* a series of essays written to convince the states to ratify the Constitution. Later, however, the two men would become bitter political enemies.

James Madison took the floor to speak at the Constitutional Convention 200 times.

the United States, George Washington, asked James Madison first to be a **diplomat** and then secretary of state. James Madison refused both jobs. Instead, he served four terms in the U.S. House of Representatives, one of the two houses of Congress. Congress met in New York, the nation's capital at the time.

Madison was a leader in Congress. Other politicians had developed a deep respect for this quiet thinker with the small voice and big ideas. He proposed the first departments of the federal government. These dealt with issues of war, finance, and **foreign affairs.** He introduced the act that created a national court system. He also introduced the act proposing the first **amendments** to the Constitution. Those that passed are known as the **Bill of Rights.** They say that all Americans have basic rights, including the right to free speech, the right to assemble, and the right to worship as they please. He introduced those amendments to the Constitution on June 8, 1789.

While Madison was serving in Congress, Thomas Jefferson returned to the United States from France. He had spent the last five years there as a diplomat. Madison and Jefferson had written to each other often while Jefferson was away. They were pleased that they could finally talk face-to-face. By 1792, the nation's politicians had divided into two **political parties.** Jefferson and Madison led the **Republican Party** (also called the Democratic-Republican Party). They often argued angrily with members of the **Federalist Party,** led by Alexander Hamilton.

The first 10 amendments to the U.S. Constitution are known as the Bill of Rights (left). James Madison was the person who proposed these important amendments to Congress.

Madison remained soft-spoken, but he was now used to public speaking.

One thing the two parties argued about was what sort of relations the United States should have with France and England. In 1789, the French had their

James Madison and Thomas Jefferson created a code so they could write secret letters to one another.

Dolley Madison was a bright, charming woman who was famous for the parties she gave.

own revolution and removed their king from power. Now they wanted to overthrow other governments that were led by kings and queens. They declared war on England. Madison and many other Republicans thought Americans should fight with France because they had signed an agreement saying they would. Federalists wanted to side with England. But President Washington decided the United States should remain **neutral.**

During this time, James Madison made a change in his personal life. In 1794, he married a widow named Dolley Payne Todd. Dolley was a friendly and energetic woman, and Madison loved her deeply.

Madison remained intensely involved in politics until George Washington left office at the end of his second term. George Washington was always very opposed to the formation of political parties in the United States. His vice president, John Adams, however, became a Federalist. Adams was elected the second president of the United States.

At that point, James Madison left Congress to retire. He and Dolley moved to Montpelier, where they added rooms and decorated the mansion. But James Madison soon became so angry about new laws Congress passed that he returned to politics. He was infuriated by the **Alien** and **Sedition** Acts. The supporters of these acts believed they would keep the country safe from spies or dangerous talk against the government.

There were three Alien Acts. Two of them could be used to make foreigners leave the country. Madison did not like the idea that newcomers could be forced to leave even if they had done nothing wrong. The third act made foreigners wait longer to become American citizens. Madison called this law "a monster."

Madison hated the Sedition Act even more. It said Americans could not criticize the government. Madison thought this was dangerous. He explained why in a paper he wrote called "The Virginia Resolves."

Dolley Madison's father was a farmer who hated slavery. He finally freed his slaves, which made it impossible to run his farm. He had to sell his land and move his wife and nine children to a small house in Philadelphia.

21

In this 1798 cartoon, the Federalists and Republicans in Congress are shown fighting about the Alien and Sedition Acts. Federalists believed these acts would prevent enemies from harming the United States. Republicans believed these acts denied the rights guaranteed by the Constitution.

He argued that the Acts were unconstitutional, which meant that they ignored the laws of the Constitution. The Sedition Act, for example, took away Americans' freedom of speech, even though the Bill of Rights guaranteed it.

Madison thought the Alien and Sedition Acts threatened the Constitution and even the country itself. When John Adams ran for a second term in 1800, Madison fought against his reelection. He wanted to be sure another Federalist would not lead the country, so he helped his good friend Thomas Jefferson become the nation's third president.

DOLLEY MADISON

In 1794, James Madison married a widow named Dolley Payne Todd. He was 43, and she was 26. Dolley Madison had been raised in the Quaker religion. This meant not only that she went to Quaker meetings—or church services—but also that she wore only plain clothes and did not attend parties or dances. But after her first husband died, Dolley stopped following Quaker ways. She started buying fancy clothes. She especially loved hats. In Washington, D.C., she became a popular hostess. In fact, it was Dolley who established the role that future first ladies would play in their husbands' careers. She threw exciting parties that people loved to attend. Her guests liked to listen to her smart and witty discussions. She always had something to say, and she laughed a lot. Dolley was six inches taller than her husband. Compared to her, Madison seemed especially small and quiet. Nevertheless, he always appreciated her lively qualities.

Dolley Madison would outlive her husband. After his death, leaders in government kept in touch with her, and first ladies asked her for advice. She decided to return to live in Washington. Although Dolley was almost 70 by that time, the people of the nation's capital found her just as charming as ever.

CHAPTER THREE

A NEW WAR

In 1800, Thomas Jefferson was elected president. When it came time for him to choose his cabinet, Jefferson asked James Madison to become secretary of state. Madison agreed to move to the nation's new capital, Washington, D.C., and fill this position. This was what he would do until 1808. Now he was in charge of the country's foreign affairs. This would be a difficult job because the United States had problems with both France and England at the time.

France and England both wanted to limit America's trade with other countries. For years, the British stopped American ships, especially those bound for France, and made the captains hand over their cargo. Then in June of 1807, a British warship attacked an American ship. The British killed one American sailor and captured three more, claiming that they were **deserters** from the British Navy. Madison and Jefferson did not want to go to war. They sent diplomats to try to find a solution, but nothing worked.

In December of 1807, Congress passed the **Embargo** Act. It said American ships could not transport goods to England—or anywhere else in

Europe. European ships could not enter American ports either. Jefferson and Madison—who supported the Act—hoped this might force France and England to leave American ships alone. They thought the Europeans would lose money without American goods. Eventually, they would want the goods so badly they would agree to stop bothering American ships.

The Embargo Act did hurt France and England, but it made Americans lose money, too. They could not sell the things they made or grew. Grains and other goods spoiled in storage before they could be sold, and farmers lost a lot of money. Sailors and shipbuilders also lost their jobs because American ships no longer

During James Madison's term as secretary of state the United States acquired the Louisiana Purchase, which almost doubled the nation's size.

When Jefferson was president, the British began stopping American ships at sea. They kidnapped U.S. sailors and forced them to join the British navy. This led to the Embargo Act of 1807.

25

As secretary of state, Madison was in charge of the nation's foreign affairs.

When he became president, James Madison had more experience in public office than any of the previous three presidents.

sailed across the Atlantic Ocean. Worst of all, smugglers sneaked goods out of the country illegally. This meant that some American goods did make it to Europe. Many Americans became very angry.

Finally, Congress ended the Embargo Act. American ships again would be allowed to transport goods abroad, but English and French ships were still not allowed to come into American ports.

In 1808, Thomas Jefferson neared the end of his second term in office. He decided he did not want to run again. Instead, in keeping with Jefferson's wishes, James Madison ran as the Republican **candidate.** It did not seem at all sure that he would win. But over time, he won the support of more and more Americans. In February of 1809, the election results were announced in Congress. Hundreds of people crowded in to hear the news. James Madison had won!

His **inauguration** was held in March on a warm, sunny day. Ten thousand people watched as he took the oath of office in his quiet, calm voice. Then he made a short speech. He swore to uphold peace as long as possible. But he also promised to go to war if the nation was threatened.

That night, he and his wife threw a fancy ball. On March 11, they moved into the presidential mansion, which Dolley Madison redecorated with satin and velvet curtains and huge mirrors. Washington leaders admired her charm and enjoyed her famous parties.

James Madison adored his wife and loved to see her excited and happy, but he was quiet at the parties. He still worried about problems with England. The English continued to stop American ships and kidnap their sailors. Madison wrote many official letters protesting such actions. England still refused to treat the United States fairly. This problem took up most of Madison's time during his first two years in office.

In the fall of 1811, James and Dolley returned to Washington, D.C., after a long summer vacation at Montpelier. A new session of Congress started in November. Madison sent a message that asked the

In 1813, James Madison almost died after he came down with yellow fever.

James Madison had two vice presidents, both of whom died while in office.

This political cartoon shows a merchant trying to smuggle goods out of the country during the Embargo Act. He is snapped by a turtle that represents federal authorities. The smuggler says "Oh, this cursed Ograbme!" "Ograbme" is "embargo" spelled backwards.

During the War of 1812, the U.S.S. Constitution *won more battles than any other American ship. Here it is shown in its victory over the* Guerrière. *Today "Old Ironsides," as the* Constitution *is known, is docked in Boston Harbor.*

lawmakers to get ready. He believed war was coming. They agreed and voted to spend money to improve the nation's weak military. They also prepared to buy more weapons and recruit more soldiers and sailors.

Madison sent one last appeal to England for peace, but he received no reply. On June 18, 1812, he asked Congress to declare war, and it agreed. At first, the war went badly for the Americans. It seemed almost certain that the United States would be defeated, and its independence was at risk. America might become part of England again if it lost the war.

As Madison's first term came to an end, the nation was divided. Federalists complained about "Mr. Madison's War." They seemed to have forgotten the problems England had caused. But the Federalists did not win the next presidential election.

In 1813, Madison was reelected and entered his second term as president. Then the American navy started to win battles. The greatest victory came on Lake Erie when Captain Oliver Perry captured an entire British squadron. Still, the British kept fighting.

In May of 1814, British ships sailed close to Washington, D.C. Madison knew the city soon would be under attack. When his generals did not do enough to get ready, Madison himself rode out to prepare the army to fight. On August 22, residents of Washington began to flee. Madison ordered that important documents, such as the Declaration of Independence, be moved out of the city and hidden.

The president camped with the soldiers. Dolley stayed in the presidential mansion, but she packed the things she loved best, including a valuable painting of President Washington. She prepared to take these items to safety when the British arrived. She used spy glasses to watch other people leave the city. She knew she would soon have to do the same. On August 23, James went to see Dolley. They did not get to spend much time together. That very night, he received an urgent message: "The enemy are in full march on Washington."

Madison returned to the army the next day. Dolley finally fled the city early that evening, just before the

James and Dolley Madison never had any children together. Dolley had two sons with her first husband, but the younger one, along with her first husband, died during an epidemic of yellow fever when Dolley was just 25 years old.

Dolley Madison's sister married a Supreme Court justice at the White House. It was the first wedding to be held there.

After the president's mansion was set on fire, only the walls remained. They were blackened by smoke, so workers painted them white. It was then that people first began calling the president's home the "White House." This finally became the official name of the mansion when Theodore Roosevelt was president.

British arrived. Their soldiers went through public buildings, burning furniture and smashing things. At about 10:30, they came to the president's mansion and plundered it, stealing and ruining things as they moved from room to room. Finally, they set fire to it. A big thunderstorm broke over the city the next morning. The rain put out the blaze and many other fires around the city. It also sent the British back to their ships.

From there, the British sailed to Baltimore, where they planned to launch their next attack. But the Americans won an important battle at Fort McHenry, which had been built to guard the city of Baltimore. At the same time, American ships won another victory on Lake Champlain. Madison sent representatives to England, hoping to convince the English king to end

On August 24, 1814, British forces under the command of Major General Ross seized Washington. Citizens, including the first lady, fled the capital to escape attack.

Dolley Madison rescued important papers as well as a famous portrait of George Washington before fleeing the White House during the British invasion of Washington, D.C.

the war. Even though it still seemed possible Great Britain could win the war, Madison knew the people of England were tired of it.

Finally, a peace treaty was signed on December 24, 1814. Because it took a very long time for news to travel across the Atlantic Ocean, soldiers in America did not know about the treaty for a while. They fought on. Future president Andrew Jackson was then a general in the army. He and his soldiers won a final battle in New Orleans in January 1815. Soon after, news of peace arrived from Europe. The war was over.

Ice cream was served in the White House for the first time while James Madison was president.

THE WHITE HOUSE ABLAZE

One of the saddest moments in American history occurred on August 24, 1814. British troops marched into Washington, D.C. They wanted to injure Americans' pride, so they planned to destroy the nation's capital. A spy told them which buildings belonged to the federal government. They went from one building to another, destroying them. Finally, they reached the presidential mansion. The soldiers walked in the front door. Everyone had run away, and there was no one left to keep them out of the mansion.

Dolley Madison and her servants had planned a large dinner party before they realized how close the British were. The meal had been cooked and was waiting on the table for the American guests who never came. Instead, the British soldiers took advantage of the situation. They sat down and devoured the feast. After dinner, they went through the house and stole or destroyed many beautiful things. When they finished wrecking the house, they set it on fire. One witness recalled that "the whole building was wrapt in flames." Rain put out the fire before the mansion burned completely, but the inside was ruined.

The painting above shows the state of the White House after the fire. When the president and first lady returned, the building was just a shell, and they could not live there. It was fully restored during James Monroe's presidency.

CHAPTER FOUR

HONORED LEADER

Peace came to the United States in the middle of James Madison's second term. The War of 1812 ended and Americans no longer feared that their country would be invaded. The independence of the United States was now firmly established. Americans, as a whole, felt calm and happy. The country appeared strong. The United States had not won or lost any land fighting the War of 1812. It had, however, won respect from other nations. England now treated the United States as an equal.

James Madison was regarded as a hero. Americans praised him for his role in winning the war. People tended to forget that many had criticized him for starting the war in the first place. One thing they did remember was that even when he was criticized, he always wanted Americans to be able to speak freely.

Late in life, Madison helped Jefferson create the University of Virginia.

After he left the presidency, Madison was happy to return to Montpelier (above) to farm and spend time with his family.

When the war ended, Madison took a vacation. He went home to Montpelier for a little while. He was an old man and the war had made him especially tired. But soon he and Dolley returned to Washington. He spent the last year and a half of his term helping the nation recover from the war. By now, the country was ready to talk about making some improvements, such as building roads and canals. James Madison took part in the debate. He knew that the United States was growing and believed that the country did in fact need better transportation. But he did not want the government's bank to pay for those improvements. In one of his last acts as president, he vetoed the act that would have allowed this to happen.

In 1817, James Madison finished his second term as president. James Monroe, who had served as Madison's secretary of state and secretary of war, became the next president. Madison was glad to leave office. By now he had reached the age of 66. He was ready to spend time farming and be with his family and friends. The Madisons went back to Montpelier, this time for good. Dolley Madison entertained friends and gardened. James Madison experimented with new crops. Sometimes he visited his old friend Thomas Jefferson.

Madison enjoyed having time to devote to his family, friends, and books. His interest in politics never ended, however. In 1828, the country suffered from what historians call the Nullification Crisis. South Carolina decided it would not obey certain laws passed by the U.S. Congress. Madison picked up his pen to explain exactly why the states had to respect the federal government. He still thought Americans should try harder to preserve the Union than to protect the rights of individual states. In 1829, he helped write a new constitution for Virginia.

As an old man, Madison suffered from **rheumatism.** His fingers became so twisted, he could hardly hold a pen. But he still dictated letters and notes to Dolley about what had happened at the Constitutional Convention. His mind remained

The term "Uncle Sam" was first used to mean the United States government during the War of 1812. The name came from "Uncle Sam" Wilson, who was a supplier of meat to the army. Wilson was reliable, honest, and devoted to his country. People soon used his nickname to refer to the U.S. government.

active until the very end. He suffered a final illness in the summer of 1836, which resulted in his peaceful death on June 28.

Long after he left public office, James Madison remained a popular figure. People admired him as one of the founding fathers. They remembered that he was president when the nation fought bravely in the War of 1812. Today Americans are still inspired by Madison's final message to his countrymen: "The advice nearest to my heart … is that the Union of the States be cherished." James Madison had devoted his life to keeping the nation strong and united.

Madison seldom left Montpelier after he retired. But in 1829, he traveled to Richmond, Virginia, to help write a new constitution for the state. He is shown here speaking to other state leaders at the convention.

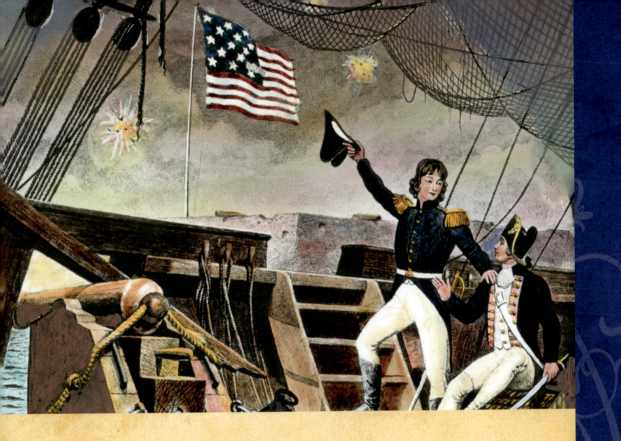

THE STAR-SPANGLED BANNER

During the War of 1812, Fort McHenry was very important because it guarded the entrance to Baltimore harbor. The fort's commander wanted a huge flag to fly over it, one that the enemy could see from afar. Such giant flags were often flown at American forts as a symbol of national pride.

The British went on to Baltimore after they captured Washington, D.C., in August of 1814. They started to bomb Fort McHenry on the morning of September 13. The bombardment continued throughout the rainy night. One person who watched from a ship eight miles away was a lawyer named Francis Scott Key. He was anxious to see if the fort had made it through the night and used a telescope to look for the flag. He saw the huge banner flying. It had been raised as the British retreated. Key was so excited that he immediately wrote a long poem about it. Soon it was set to the tune of a popular song. "The Star-Spangled Banner" eventually became the U.S. national anthem. The huge flag goes by the same name and is on display at the Museum of American History in Washington, D.C. It is so large that it has to be hung on a wall two stories high.

Time Line

| **1750** | **1760** | **1770** | | **1780** |

1751
James Madison is born on March 16 in western Virginia.

1762
James Madison leaves home to go to boarding school.

1767
Madison returns to Montpelier, his family's plantation, to study with a tutor whom his father has hired.

1769
Madison leaves Virginia to attend the College of New Jersey.

1771
Madison finishes college in just two years instead of the four years it takes most students. Unfortunately, he has made himself so sick by studying late into the night that he cannot attend graduation.

1772
In April, Madison goes home to Montpelier. He helps his father run the plantation and teaches his younger brothers and sisters.

1774
Madison buys land from his father, which gives him the right to vote and run for office. He is elected to the local Committee of Safety.

1775
The first battles of the Revolutionary War are fought.

Madison is not strong enough to join the army but contributes to the cause in other ways.

1776
Madison attends the Virginia Revolutionary Convention, which writes a constitution for the new state.

1777
Madison joins the Virginia Governor's Council. His lifelong friendship with Thomas Jefferson begins.

1779
Madison is elected to the Second Continental Congress.

1783
When Madison's term in Congress ends, he retires to Montpelier.

1784
Madison is elected to Virginia's state legislature.

1785
James Madison proposes that delegates from every state meet at a convention to discuss commerce. The delegates meet again in 1787 to change the Articles of Confederation. They then decide to replace the Articles with a new constitution.

1787
On May 14, the Constitutional Convention opens. The delegates sign the Constitution in September, but it still needs to be ratified by at least nine states.

1788
Nine states ratify the U.S. Constitution.

1789
The new federal government is created. Madison is elected to the House of Representatives. He helps convince other representatives to add amendments to the Constitution, which later become known as the Bill of Rights.

1791

The Bill of Rights, which Madison introduced into Congress in 1789, is ratified.

1794

James Madison marries Dolley Payne Todd, a widow.

1797

Madison leaves Congress when President Washington leaves office.

1798

Congress passes the Alien and Sedition Acts, which Madison believes are wrong. He returns to politics to combat what he believes are unconstitutional laws.

1800

Madison helps Thomas Jefferson get elected the third president of the United States. Jefferson names Madison as his secretary of state.

1807

President Jefferson asks Congress to pass the Embargo Act, which stops American trade with European powers. Although the act is meant to hurt England and France, many Americans lose business because of it. The embargo is ended two years later.

1809

James Madison is sworn in as the fourth president of the United States.

1812

The War of 1812 breaks out between England and the United States.

1813

Madison begins his second term as president. The war continues.

1814

On August 24, British troops invade Washington, D.C., and burn many public buildings, including the president's mansion. England finally agrees to peace on December 24, but battles continue in the United States for another month.

1815

On January 8, the Americans beat the British at the Battle of New Orleans.

1817

Madison's term as president ends. He and Dolley return to Montpelier after the new president, James Monroe, is inaugurated.

1828

After South Carolina refuses to obey certain federal laws, Madison again expresses his belief that states must respect the national government.

1829

Madison writes a new constitution for Virginia.

1836

Madison dies on June 28.

GLOSSARY

alien (AY-lee-un) An alien is a person who is not a citizen of the country where he or she lives. Congress proposed the Alien Acts to keep the country safe from foreign spies.

amendments (uh-MEND-mentz) Amendments are changes or additions made to the Constitution or other documents. Madison introduced the first amendments to the Constitution (the Bill of Rights).

Articles of Confederation (AR-teh-kelz OF kun-fed-uh-RAY-shun) The Articles of Confederation made up the first plan for a central U.S. government. Many leaders believed the Articles of Confederation did not create a strong enough government.

Bill of Rights (BILL OF RYTZ) The Bill of Rights are the first 10 amendments to the U.S. Constitution. In the Bill of Rights, the government promises to protect the basic or natural rights of the people, such as freedom of religion and freedom of speech.

candidate (KAN-deh-dut) Candidates are people who are running in an election. Several candidates run for president every four years.

checks and balances (CHEKS AND BAL-en-sez) Checks and balances are the limits the Constitution places on branches of the federal government. For example, the president is commander in chief of the army, but only Congress can declare a war. Checks and balances prevent any one branch from becoming too powerful.

commerce (KOM-urss) Commerce is the buying and selling of large amounts of goods between different places. Representatives from each state argued about commerce.

constitution (kon-stih-TOO-shun) A constitution is the set of rules that a government has to follow. Madison wrote most of the U.S. Constitution.

Continental Congress (kon-tuh-NEN-tul KONG-gris) The Continental Congress was the group of men who governed the United States during and after the Revolution. Madison was a member of the Continental Congress.

convention (kun-VEN-shun) A convention is a meeting. Members of the Constitutional Convention created the U.S. Constitution.

delegate (DEL-eh-get) A delegate is a person elected to take part in something. Delegates from each state met at the Constitutional Convention to discuss the federal government.

deserters (dih-ZER-turz) Deserters are people who leave something that they shouldn't leave, such as the military. The British searched American ships for deserters from their navy.

diplomat (DIP-luh-mat) A diplomat is a government official whose job is to represent a country in discussions with other countries. Thomas Jefferson served as a diplomat to France.

embargo (em-BAR-goh) An embargo stops one country from selling its goods to another country. The United States began an embargo against England in 1807.

epilepsy (EP-uh-lep-see) Epilepsy is a disease that affects a person's nervous system. It can cause someone to suffer from seizures and become unconscious.

executive (eg-ZEK-yuh-tiv) An executive manages things or makes decisions. The executive branch of the U.S. government includes the president and the cabinet members.

federal (FED-ur-ul) Federal means having to do with the central government of the United States, rather than a state or city government. Madison believed states had to obey federal laws.

Federalist Party (FED-ur-ul-ist PAR-tee)
The Federalist political party in Madison's time was similar to today's Republican Party. Federalists believed that a few well-educated landowners should run the nation.

foreign affairs (FOR-un uh-FAIRZ)
Foreign affairs are matters involving other (foreign) countries. Madison suggested that a government department should be created to deal with foreign affairs.

ideal (eye-DEEL) An ideal is a model or idea of the best something could be. Madison believed in the ideal of religious freedom.

inauguration (ih-naw-gyuh-RAY-shun) An inauguration is the ceremony that takes place when a new president begins a term. Madison's inauguration was held on March 9, 1809.

judicial (joo-DISH-ul) Judicial means relating to courts of law. The judicial branch of the federal government includes its courts and judges.

legislative (LEJ-uh-slay-tiv) Legislative means having to do with the making of laws. The legislative branch of the U.S. government is Congress.

militia (muh-LISH-uh) A militia is a volunteer army, made up of citizens who have trained as soldiers. Virginia had a militia for times of emergency.

neutral (NOO-trul) If people are neutral, they do not take sides. President Washington believed the United States should remain neutral in the affairs of other nations.

plantation (plan-TAY-shun) A plantation is a large farm or group of farms. Montpelier was the name of James Madison's plantation.

political parties (puh-LIT-uh-kul PAR-teez) Political parties are groups of people who share similar ideas about how to run a government. By 1792, the nation's politicians had begun to divide into political parties.

politics (PAWL-uh-tiks) Politics refers to the actions and practices of the government. Madison and his college friends talked about politics.

ratification (rat-uh-fih-KAY-shun) Ratification is approval by a group of people. After the Constitution was written, people from the states ratified it by voting in its favor.

representative (rep-ree-ZEN-tuh-tiv) A representative is someone who attends a meeting, having agreed to speak or act for others. American colonists believed they should have a representative in the British government.

Republican Party (ree-PUB-lih-ken PAR-tee) The Republican Party (also called the Democratic-Republican Party) of Madison's time was similar to today's Democratic Party. Members of the party believed that more citizens should be given the right to vote and take part in the federal government.

revolution (rev-uh-LOO-shun) A revolution is something (such as a war) that causes a complete change in government. The American Revolution was a war fought between the United States and England.

rheumatism (ROO-muh-tih-zim) Rheumatism is a condition that causes pain in muscles and joints. Madison suffered from rheumatism.

sedition (suh-DIH-shun) Sedition is something said or written, such as a newspaper article, that causes people to rebel against the government. The Sedition Act said Americans could not criticize government.

THE UNITED STATES GOVERNMENT

The United States government is divided into three equal branches: the executive, the legislative, and the judicial. This division helps prevent abuses of power because each branch has to answer to the other two. No one branch can become too powerful.

EXECUTIVE BRANCH

PRESIDENT
VICE PRESIDENT
DEPARTMENTS

The job of the executive branch is to enforce the laws. It is headed by the president, who serves as the spokesperson for the United States around the world. The president signs bills into law and appoints important officials such as federal judges. He or she is also the commander in chief of the U.S. military. The president is assisted by the vice president, who takes over if the president dies or cannot carry out the duties of the office.

The executive branch also includes various departments, each focused on a specific topic. They include the Defense Department, the Justice Department, and the Agriculture Department. The department heads, along with other officials such as the vice president, serve as the president's closest advisers, called the cabinet.

LEGISLATIVE BRANCH

CONGRESS
Senate and
House of Representatives

The job of the legislative branch is to make the laws. It consists of Congress, which is divided into two parts: the Senate and the House of Representatives. The Senate has 100 members, and the House of Representatives has 435 members. Each state has two senators. The number of representatives a state has varies depending on the state's population.

Besides making laws, Congress also passes budgets and enacts taxes. In addition, it is responsible for declaring war, maintaining the military, and regulating trade with other countries.

JUDICIAL BRANCH

SUPREME COURT
COURTS OF APPEALS
DISTRICT COURTS

The job of the judicial branch is to interpret the laws. It consists of the nation's federal courts. Trials are held in district courts. During trials, judges must decide what laws mean and how they apply. Courts of appeals review the decisions made in district courts.

The nation's highest court is the Supreme Court. If someone disagrees with a court of appeals ruling, he or she can ask the Supreme Court to review it. The Supreme Court may refuse. The Supreme Court makes sure that decisions and laws do not violate the Constitution.

CHOOSING THE PRESIDENT

It may seem odd, but American voters don't elect the president directly. Instead, the president is chosen using what is called the Electoral College.

Each state gets as many votes in the Electoral College as its combined total of senators and representatives in Congress. For example, Iowa has two senators and five representatives, so it gets seven electoral votes. Although the District of Columbia does not have any voting members in Congress, it gets three electoral votes. Usually, the candidate who wins the most votes in any given state receives all of that state's electoral votes.

To become president, a candidate must get more than half of the Electoral College votes. There are a total of 538 votes in the Electoral College, so a candidate needs 270 votes to win. If nobody receives 270 Electoral College votes, the House of Representatives chooses the president.

With the Electoral College system, the person who receives the most votes nationwide does not always receive the most electoral votes. This happened most recently in 2000, when Al Gore received half a million more national votes than George W. Bush. Bush became president because he had more Electoral College votes.

THE WHITE HOUSE

The White House is the official home of the president of the United States. It is located at 1600 Pennsylvania Avenue NW in Washington, D.C. In 1792, a contest was held to select the architect who would design the president's home. James Hoban won. Construction took eight years.

The first president, George Washington, never lived in the White House. The second president, John Adams, moved into the house in 1800, though the inside was not yet complete. During the War of 1812, British soldiers burned down much of the White House. It was rebuilt several years later.

The White House was changed through the years. Porches were added, and President Theodore Roosevelt added the West Wing. President William Taft changed the shape of the presidential office, making it into the famous Oval Office. While Harry Truman was president, the old house was discovered to be structurally weak. All the walls were reinforced with steel, and the rooms were rebuilt.

Today, the White House has 132 rooms (including 35 bathrooms), 28 fireplaces, and 3 elevators. It takes 570 gallons of paint to cover the outside of the six-story building. The White House provides the president with many ways to relax. It includes a putting green, a jogging track, a swimming pool, a tennis court, and beautifully landscaped gardens. The White House also has a movie theater, a billiard room, and a one-lane bowling alley.

PRESIDENTIAL PERKS

The job of president of the United States is challenging. It is probably one of the most stressful jobs in the world. Because of this, presidents are paid well, though not nearly as well as the leaders of large corporations. In 2007, the president earned $400,000 a year. Presidents also receive extra benefits that make the demanding job a little more appealing.

★ **Camp David:** In the 1940s, President Franklin D. Roosevelt chose this heavily wooded spot in the mountains of Maryland to be the presidential retreat, where presidents can relax. Even though it is a retreat, world business is conducted there. Most famously, President Jimmy Carter met with Middle Eastern leaders at Camp David in 1978. The result was a peace agreement between Israel and Egypt.

★ *Air Force One:* The president flies on a jet called *Air Force One*. It is a Boeing 747-200B that has been modified to meet the president's needs.

Air Force One is the size of a large home. It is equipped with a dining room, sleeping quarters, a conference room, and office space. It also has two kitchens that can provide food for up to 50 people.

★ **The Secret Service:** While not the most glamorous of the president's perks, the Secret Service is one of the most important. The Secret Service is a group of highly trained agents who protect the president and the president's family.

★ **The Presidential State Car:** The presidential limousine is a stretch Cadillac DTS.

It has been armored to protect the president in case of attack. Inside the plush car are a foldaway desk, an entertainment center, and a communications console.

★ **The Food:** The White House has five chefs who will make any food the president wants. The White House also has an extensive wine collection.

★ **Retirement:** A former president receives a pension, or retirement pay, of just under $180,000 a year. Former presidents also receive Secret Service protection for the rest of their lives.

FACTS

QUALIFICATIONS

To run for president, a candidate must

- ★ be at least 35 years old
- ★ be a citizen who was born in the United States
- ★ have lived in the United States for 14 years

TERM OF OFFICE

A president's term of office is four years.
No president can stay in office for more than two terms.

ELECTION DATE

The presidential election takes place every four years on the first Tuesday of November.

INAUGURATION DATE

Presidents are inaugurated on January 20.

OATH OF OFFICE

I do solemnly swear I will faithfully execute the office of the President of the United States and will to the best of my ability preserve, protect, and defend the Constitution of the United States.

WRITE A LETTER TO THE PRESIDENT

One of the best things about being a U.S. citizen is that Americans get to participate in their government. They can speak out if they feel government leaders aren't doing their jobs. They can also praise leaders who are going the extra mile. Do you have something you'd like the president to do? Should the president worry more about the environment and encourage people to recycle? Should the government spend more money on our schools? You can write a letter to the president to say how you feel!

1600 Pennsylvania Avenue
Washington, D.C. 20500
You can even send an e-mail to: president@whitehouse.gov

BOOKS

Ashby, Ruth. *James and Dolley Madison.* Milwaukee, WI: World Almanac Library, 2005.

Fritz, Jean. *The Great Little Madison.* New York: Putnam, 1989.

Hakim, Joy. *From Colonies to Country.* 3rd edition. New York: Oxford University Press, 2003.

Mitchell, Barbara. *Father of the Constitution: A Story About James Madison.* Minneapolis: Carolrhoda Books, 2004.

Robinet, Harriette Gillem. *Washington City Is Burning.* New York: Atheneum, 1996.

Swain, Gwenyth. *Declaring Freedom: A Look at the Declaration of Independence, the Bill of Rights, and the Constitution.* Minneapolis: Lerner Publications, 2004.

VIDEOS

The American President. DVD, VHS (Alexandria, VA: PBS Home Video, 2000).

The History Channel Presents The President. DVD (New York: A & E Home Video, 2005).

Just the Facts—United States Constitution and Bill of Rights. DVD, VHS (Thousand Oaks CA: Goldhil Home Media, 2004).

National Geographic's Inside the White House. DVD (Washington, D.C.: National Geographic Video, 2003).

INTERNET SITES

Visit our Web page for lots of links about James Madison and other U.S. presidents:

http://www.childsworld.com/links

Note to Parents, Teachers, and Librarians: We routinely verify our Web links to make sure they are safe, active sites—so encourage your readers to check them out!

INDEX